P9-BYW-058

599.7357   Sattler, Helen
SAT   Giraffes, the   ey
           sentinels of
11A8850   the Savannas

$14.95

DATE		
JAN 1 4 1992		
~~2 4~~		
OCT 24		
JAN 0 4 1996		

GEORGE ROGERS CLARK
LIBRARY MEDIA CENTER

© THE BAKER & TAYLOR CO.

GIRAFFES,

the Sentinels of the Savannas

ALSO BY HELEN RONEY SATTLER

Baby Dinosaurs
The Book of Eagles
Dinosaurs of North America
The Illustrated Dinosaur Dictionary
Recipes for Art and Craft Materials
Sharks, the Super Fish
Train Whistles
Tyrannosaurus Rex and Its Kin: The Mesozoic Monsters
Whales, the Nomads of the Sea

ILLUSTRATED BY CHRISTOPHER SANTORO

Hominids: A Look Back at Our Ancestors
Pterosaurs, the Flying Reptiles

GIRAFFES,
the Sentinels of the Savannas

BY HELEN RONEY SATTLER

ILLUSTRATED BY CHRISTOPHER SANTORO

LOTHROP, LEE & SHEPARD BOOKS
NEW YORK

599.73
SAT

ACKNOWLEDGMENTS

I would like to express my deepest appreciation to Hugh Davis, former director of the Tulsa Zoo, for reading the completed manuscript and checking the drawings for accuracy. I also extend special thanks to Dr. John Harris, Chief Curator, Division of Earth Sciences, The Museum of Natural History of Los Angeles, California, for his invaluable assistance with the fossil giraffids, and to Ken Stott, former curator of the San Diego Zoo, for sharing information about giraffes and his·personal experiences with them. In addition to those listed in the For Further Reading section, I am indebted to the following authors for information gleaned from their books or articles in magazines or scientific journals: C. C. Balch, Peter H. Beard, Edward Bone, A. Brownlee, Maurice Burton, C. C. Churcher, F. Fraser Darling, Bernhard Grzimek, Sigmund A. Lavine, C. T. Astley Maberly, Marius Maxwell, Betty Melville, Chapman Pincer, Ronald Singer, Ken Stott, and Robert L. Van Citters.

Text copyright © 1989 by Helen Roney Sattler
Illustrations copyright © 1989 by Christopher Santoro
All rights reserved. No part of this book may be reproduced or utilized in any form or by any means, electronic or mechanical, including photocopying, recording or by any information storage and retrieval system, without permission in writing from the Publisher. Inquiries should be addressed to Lothrop, Lee & Shepard Books, a division of William Morrow & Company, Inc., 105 Madison Avenue, New York, New York 10016. Printed in the United States of America.

First Edition 1 2 3 4 5 6 7 8 9 10

Library of Congress Cataloging in Publication Data
Sattler, Helen Roney.
Giraffes, the sentinels of the Savannas / by Helen Roney Sattler.
p.   cm. Bibliography: p.   Includes index. Summary: Discusses the physical characteristics, habits, natural environment, and relationship to human beings of giraffes. Includes a glossary giving the popular and scientific name of each species and details of their size and appearance.
ISBN 0-688-08284-X. — ISBN 0-688-08285-8 (lib. bdg.)
1. Giraffes—Juvenile literature. [1. Giraffes.] I. Santoro, Christopher, ill. II. Title.
QL737.U56S28 1990 599.73'57—dc19
89-2287 CIP AC

To my nieces and nephews:
Bob, Tom, Patty, Ron, Stephen, Don, Karen,
and Peggy.
H.R.S.

To Dorothy Briley.
C.S.

Contents

Masai giraffes

I
Graceful Giants

I could tell we had entered giraffe country; the huge, twelve-inch-long hoofprints in the mud beside the road couldn't have been made by anything but a giraffe. I scanned the horizon, eager for my first glimpse of a giraffe in its own habitat. Olive-green, acorn-shaped piles of droppings indicated that one had passed this way recently.

We rounded a bend, and suddenly there, in the middle of the road, stood five elegant Masai giraffes facing us with heads together. They looked like a welcoming committee. I half expected to hear them say, "Welcome to Kenya!" But they just stood there staring at us and chewing their cuds with their mouths open. They reminded me of a group of teenagers with large wads of bubble gum.

The quintet eyed us intently as we approached, but when we were within a hundred feet of them, they scattered and galumphed off into the bush in a curious slow-motion gallop, their hind legs coming well ahead of their forelegs. Their long tails, swishing like windshield wipers, looked as if someone had tied three-foot-long tassels to them. The giraffes soon stopped, however, and turned to watch us as we passed. It was a strange feeling to be the one in the cage while they stood outside and stared in at us. I wondered, Is this how animals in zoos feel?

I have been fascinated with giraffes ever since I saw my first one in a circus parade when I was five years old. They are still my favorites at the zoo. Their sheer size, beauty, and stateliness fill me with awe. The day a female stretched her long neck across the moat separating us and looked at me with her beautiful brown, baseball-sized eyes, fringed with long dark lashes, I completely fell in love. I was determined to learn all I could about her and her kind.

At first glance, a giraffe may look awkward and impractical with its ridiculously long neck and legs. Actually, this magnificent animal is extremely graceful and in perfect control of its huge body. It is an excellent example of marvelously efficient design. That long neck is the giraffe's most important adaptation to its enviroment. Just as the whale and shark found their niches in the ocean, the long-necked giraffe found its niche in the sea of grass and bush along the edge of the savannas of Africa. Its long neck permits it to browse where few other modern animals can.

Although giraffes in zoos are impressive, they give no indication of their real power and grace. Giraffes are obviously built for speed and wide-open spaces. Many scientists study giraffes in the national parks and game reserves of Kenya, because they can find more than one kind of

giraffe there. I wanted to see what these magnificent creatures were like on the open plains of their homeland, so that is where I went.

I was not disappointed. A free-roaming giraffe seen for the first time, whether in the middle of the road or across open country, is a memorable sight. To be in the middle of a herd of seventy-five reticulated giraffes, as I was in the Samburu Game Reserve, is sensational. No captive animal could ever compare with those on the savanna. They don't get enough exercise in captivity to develop their muscles, and they lose many other special adaptations because they no longer need them. Giraffes on the open range have great rippling muscles and are as graceful as ballet dancers. When they run, they seem to float through the air.

Giraffes have had a long association with humans. They lived side by side with our earliest ancestors. Thousands of years ago ancient tribesmen decorated their caves with pictures of them. Ancient Egyptians presented them as gifts to kings. Today humans have become a threat to these fascinating animals, and giraffes rarely allow people to get closer than a hundred feet to them. It is important that we continue to share our world with these unique creatures, and to do this, we need to know more about them.

11

Zarafa zelteni, primitive giraffid from the Miocene epoch

2
What Is a Giraffe?

The giraffe's long neck and legs are the most obvious features that make it different from all other animals. They make the giraffe the tallest living creature and are responsible for its very successful adaptation to its environment. However, there are other important characteristics that separate giraffes from other animals. Not all members of the giraffe family have had long necks.

The scientific name for the giraffe is *Giraffa camelopardalis*. The genus name, *Giraffa*, comes from the Arabian word *zirafah* (zih-RAF-ah), which means "the tallest of animals" or "one that walks very fast." The species name, *camelopardalis*, comes from "camelopard," which is what the ancient Europeans called this animal because they thought it was a cross between a camel and a leopard.

Actually the giraffe's closest relatives are antelopes and deer. Scientists think all three developed from a member of the Paleomerycidae (PAY-lee-o-mer-IK-ih-dee), a family of ancient deerlike creatures, some of which had horns quite similar to those of giraffes. Like deer and antelopes as well as camels, sheep, goats, and cattle, giraffes are ungulates (UN-gyoo-lates)—hoofed animals—that have an even number of toes and chew cuds or ruminate (ROO-mih-nate).

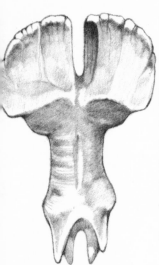

bilobed canine tooth

wedge-shaped hoof

Scientists divide related animals into families. Giraffes belong to the Giraffidae family. Members of this family are called giraffids. Giraffids are two-toed ruminating ungulates that have bilobed canine teeth (teeth that have two blades instead of one), wedge-shaped hoofs adapted for speed, and horns that are covered with skin and are present at birth. They are among the few animals that are born with horns, and they never shed them.

Giraffid fossils have been found in Spain, Hungary, Greece, Iran, northern India, Pakistan, and China, and throughout Africa. Giraffids first appeared about twenty-five million years ago. Scientists once thought that these animals originated in Europe or Asia and migrated into Africa, but the oldest known giraffids were found in northern Africa. Therefore, some scientists now think that giraffes may have evolved in Africa and spread to Eurasia about fifteen million years ago.

There are three kinds of giraffids: the Paleotraginae (PAY-lee-o-TRAG-ih-nee), the Sivatheriinae (siv-ah-THEE-ree-ih-nee), and the Giraffinae (jye-RAF-fih-nee). The Paleotraginae are the oldest group. The most primitive of them, the genus *Zarafa*, lived in northern Africa twenty million years ago during the early Miocene (MY-o-seen) epoch. Their necks were no longer than a modern deer's.

The okapi (o-KAH-pee), a close relative of the giraffe, is thought by some to be the only living descendant of the Paleotraginae giraffids. Except for their feet, long legs, bilobed canines, and skin-covered horns, okapi do not look much like giraffes. They are only half as tall, have much shorter necks, have less slope to their backs, and are colored entirely differently. They look more like the extinct *Paleotragus* (PAY-lee-o-TRAG-us), which lived in central Asia and Africa about fifteen million years ago. Because the okapi have changed so little from those that lived millions of years ago, people sometimes call them "living fossils." Unfortunately the okapi may soon be extinct, too. It lives only in the rain forests of Zaire in central Africa and is rarely seen.

The Sivatheriinae lived in Europe, Asia, and Africa from about fifteen million to five thousand years ago. They had huge bodies like those of oxen, short necks, and sturdy legs like those of cattle. Some, like *Sivatherium* (siv-ah-THEE-rih-um), had elaborate horns similar to those of a moose. This entire group of giraffids is now extinct; not one living relative remains.

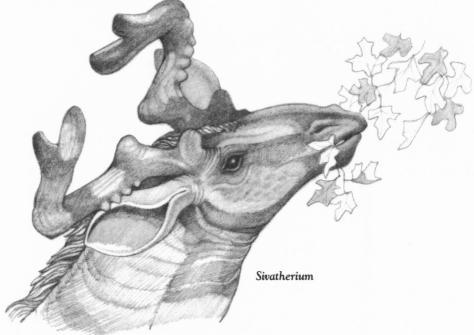

Sivatherium

The Giraffinae are long-necked giraffes. They include the modern giraffe, the only other living giraffid, and its ancestors. The oldest known giraffine, *Giraffa jumae* (JEW-me), lived in East Africa from the late Miocene to the mid-Pleistocene (PLY-steh-seen) epoch. The oldest of the Asian Giraffinae is believed to be *Giraffa priscilla*, but it is not certain that this animal is a giraffid because its canine teeth have not been found. It lived in India about ten million years ago during the Pliocene (PLY-o-seen) epoch. *Giraffa camelopardalis* appeared in Africa a million years ago during the early Pleistocene epoch and has not changed in appearance since.

Giraffinae
(shown: *Giraffa camelopardalis*)

Sivatheriinae
(shown: *Sivatherium*)

Paleotraginae
(shown: *Zarafa*)

GIRAFFID FAMILY TREE

Although only one species of *Giraffa* remains today, there are several subspecies or races, some of which are now almost extinct. Subspecies result when populations become isolated from one another. *Giraffa* subspecies differ only in minor characteristics such as color patterns, size, and number of horns. They can, and do, interbreed and herd together. While not everyone agrees, most authorities recognize nine subspecies.

Once giraffids ranged all over Africa, southern Europe, and southeastern Asia. There were no water barriers they could not cross between Eurasia and Africa. Giraffids could have migrated freely back and forth. Then altered climatic conditions made some areas unsuitable for giraffes. Those animals that could not migrate to more suitable areas died out. A few thousand years ago giraffes were plentiful in northern Africa. Then long periods of little or no rainfall caused vegetation to die and created the Sahara Desert. Giraffes that lived there moved farther to the south or died of starvation.

Today these magnificent animals exist only in a narrow belt across the center of Africa, in a small section of southern Africa, and in zoos around the world. In the past their ranges were destroyed by climatic changes. Today their problems are caused by climatic conditions, disease, and human influence. Each year large numbers are slaughtered for their skins or the hair at the end of their tails. The hair,

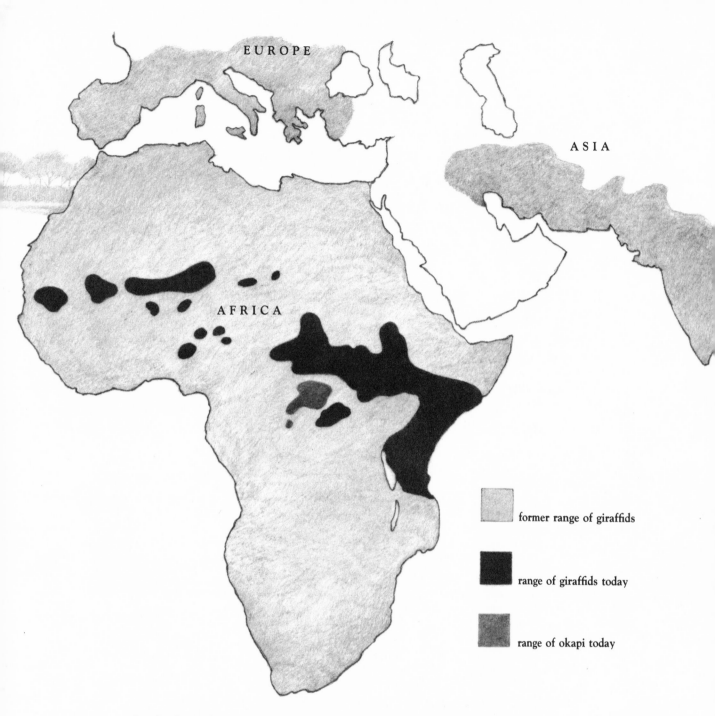

which feels like nylon cord and is thicker than the heaviest fishline, is made into bracelets. Giraffes' habitats are diminishing because of rapidly increasing human populations. Only a few giraffes remain in all of western Africa.

Fortunately, giraffes have learned to live in regions where few other animals can. It is the responsibility of humans to preserve these habitats for them before it is too late.

giraffe hair bracelet

reticulated giraffe

3
Walking Watchtowers

Three male giraffes munched contentedly on the yellow-green leaves of an acacia (ah-KAY-sha) tree by the side of the road. Gazelles and zebras grazed on the grassy areas nearby. As our minivan approached, the largest giraffe snorted, and the grazing animals streaked off into the dusk. The giraffes, however, galloped only a short distance before their curiosity got the better of them. They stopped and turned, then stood immobile, gazing with their enormous eyes at the intruders.

Although giraffes are often called timid creatures, they are not really timid but extremely wary, especially of humans. Giraffes have extraordinarily keen eyesight and can spot danger much sooner than other animals. Their range of vision is wider than that of most mammals, and they can see greater distances. A giraffe's eyes are larger than those of any other land mammal and are situated on the sides of the head atop a long, periscope-like neck.

Giraffes can detect a moving person a mile away; they probably saw our van long before we saw them. These incredibly observant creatures take notice of the slightest changes in their environment. Once a giraffe handler in the San Diego Zoo placed an ordinary thumbtack on the wall of the giraffes' dimly lit stall while they were feeding in the yard. Then he opened the stall door to let them back in. They stuck their heads in, spotted the tack immediately, and refused to enter until it was removed.

Giraffes living in the wild are alert for danger every minute. Even when feeding, at least one of the herd will be scanning the countryside. Little escapes their notice, not even a tawny lion creeping through dry grass. Zebras, ostriches, kudus, impalas, wildebeests, hartebeests, and gazelles often stay as close to these walking watchtowers as they can. Whenever a giraffe indicates something threatening is approaching, the plains animals flee instantly.

Although giraffes rely mostly on sight for spotting danger, they also hear very well. At the slightest unfamiliar sound every member of the herd turns toward the noise with its eight-inch-long ears directed forward. Young giraffes tend to rely more on hearing than do adults because they are much shorter and can't see as far.

When giraffes can't identify a sound or object, they crane their necks or walk closer to get a better view. They have an insatiable curiosity and sometimes stand on termite hills so they can see even farther. Africans claim that their curiosity is responsible for their extremely long necks.

Curiosity is believed to be a sign of intelligence, but no one knows exactly how intelligent giraffes are. Though their brains are not very large, they seem to be at least as smart as horses. Their intelligence is certainly adequate for their needs. Like all creatures, including humans, they sometimes get themselves into messes they can't figure out how to get out of, but some, at least, show a great deal of ingenuity. A female in the Manchester, England, zoo learned how to open and close the door of her house. When she wanted to be alone, she simply went inside and closed the door. Once, when a male giraffe was pestering her by pressing his unwanted attentions on her, she lured him into the stall, then ducked out and closed the door, shutting him inside.

Though wary, giraffes are peaceful animals and never bother the grass-eaters that wander through their herds. Other animals don't compete with them for food because giraffes dine on vegetation that most other animals cannot reach. These gentle giants fight only when attacked.

Besides humans, their only real enemies are lions. A lion seldom has a chance to get close enough to a healthy adult to attack it, unless the giraffe happens to be lying down, drinking, or feeding in thick bush, where its range of vision is obscured. Giraffes usually herd with anywhere from three to fifteen other giraffes, sometimes—though rarely—as many as seventy-five. They like company, possibly because there is greater safety in numbers. The more eyes and ears there are to watch and listen for danger, the better protection they have.

Females usually hang out with family groups, sharing food and often dining from the same treetop. Young males may stay with a family or join an all-bachelor group. Bachelor groups are made up of young males led by an older bull, usually the largest and strongest. Our welcoming committee was a bachelor group—one very dark older male, one light-colored teenager, and three somewhere in between.

Giraffes are rather independent creatures. Although they sometimes stay with one group for a long time, they don't always stay with the same group. Except for mothers and their young, they tend to wander about a good deal, separating from one group and joining another. But they almost always stay within one general feeding area.

Two or three hundred giraffes may live in a single home range, which can cover fifteen hundred square miles. The low bush country where most giraffes live is hot and dry much of the year. Giraffes prefer this environment because it is open and they can spot danger in plenty of time to get away. Also there is plenty of room to run in. They avoid dense forests, because forests provide too many hiding places for enemies, but they sometimes browse in wooded areas on the edge of the savannas.

These tree-browsers tend to spread out, often wandering up to twenty miles in a single day in search of food or water. A giraffe sometimes appears to be alone but is probably within hearing or sight of others. Individuals separated by as much as a mile are still able to see one another and receive warning signals.

Giraffes stay in their home area as long as there is plenty of vegetation. During the rainy seasons vegetation stays green, but during the hot, dry seasons the home area sometimes becomes overbrowsed. Then, if they can, the giraffes move or migrate to another area where there is lusher vegetation. They are unable to cross large rivers, lakes, or mountains.

Except when migrating, giraffes are rarely far from a clump of acacia trees, their favorite food. These trees grow well in the semiarid bush regions of Africa and along the edges of the savanna, which are the giraffes' favorite habitats.

reticulated giraffe drinking

4
Dining and Drinking

Giraffes are browsers. They eat shoots and leaves. They also eat fruits and seedpods. They are very fond of the fruit of the sausage tree, which looks like sausages hanging from the branches, and of maroela berries. Unfortunately, maroela berries ferment in their stomachs. When they eat too many of them, they become intoxicated. Though a drunken giraffe looks comical staggering around on its stiltlike legs, it could be in serious danger. If it fell, it might break a leg. A drunken giraffe once blundered into a river and became trapped in thick, oozing mud. If scientists hadn't rescued it, it would have drowned.

Their favorite foods are the spiny acacia (an umbrella-shaped tree with small leaves among tufts of three-inch-long thorns) and the young whistling thorn acacia. This tree gets its name from wind whistling through galls on the ends of the branches. The galls are made by stinging ants. Most browsers avoid trees that harbor stinging ants, but giraffes tend to ignore the insects.

Acacia trees grow rapidly in the savannas and would soon take over the grasslands if not kept pruned by the giraffes. When acacia trees are abundant, giraffes get quite fat. Acacia leaves are highly nutritious and moist. They contain almost everything a giraffe needs except salt and calcium. Giraffes get these minerals by licking natural salt deposits and chewing the bones of dead animals.

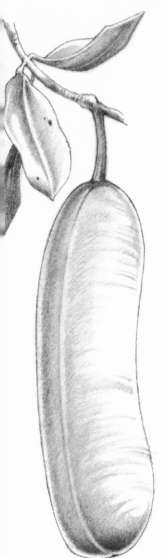

sausage tree fruit

Giraffes have enormous appetites and each day spend many hours eating. A large male can consume seventy-five pounds of food every twenty-four hours. Lots of nourishment is required to supply enough energy to operate their huge bodies. Each time a large male giraffe raises its head, it lifts 550 pounds (the combined weight of the neck and head).

Giraffes usually browse in early morning or late at night when the air is cooler and the leaves are wet with dew. Ordinarily they spend just a few minutes at each tree, choosing only the tenderest and freshest of the new growth. In daylight they select food by sight but appear to sniff it out at night.

With its six- to eight-foot-long neck, a giraffe can reach new growth at the very top of trees. The necks of giraffes have only seven vertebrae, the same number that most mammals have. The increased neck length, which evolved to allow the animals to eat nutritious soft leaves of tall trees, comes from vertebrae that have grown very long. Some of the vertebrae are more than eight inches long! (Those of a horse are four to five inches long.) A special hinge at the base of the head allows the giraffe to raise its long, slender head in a straight line with the neck. Very few animals can do that. This hinge gives the giraffe two more feet of reach.

Giraffes are dainty eaters, often sampling a single leaf from a tree. A giraffe plucks leaves off with its prehensile upper lip (the lip can grasp like a finger). In addition, it can flip out its eighteen-inch-long tongue and wrap it around choice bits too far away to reach with the upper lip. A giraffe has no front teeth in its upper jaw. It clips off leaves and small twigs by pressing the front lower incisors against the gum pad of the upper jaw.

Masai giraffes eating acacia leaves

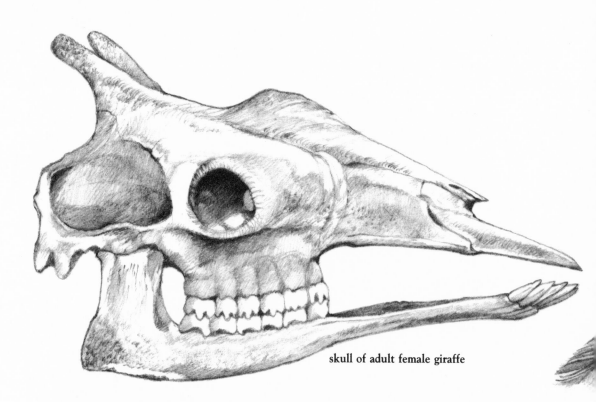

skull of adult female giraffe

Most animals avoid acacia trees because of their long thorns, but giraffes aren't bothered much by the thorns. A giraffe's mouth and snout are almost puncture-proof. It closes its slitlike nostrils when poking among thorns, and a velvety coat of very strong hair shields its upper lip. Immature thorns on new growth are soft and easily digested when mixed with the very thick, almost rubberlike saliva in the giraffe's mouth.

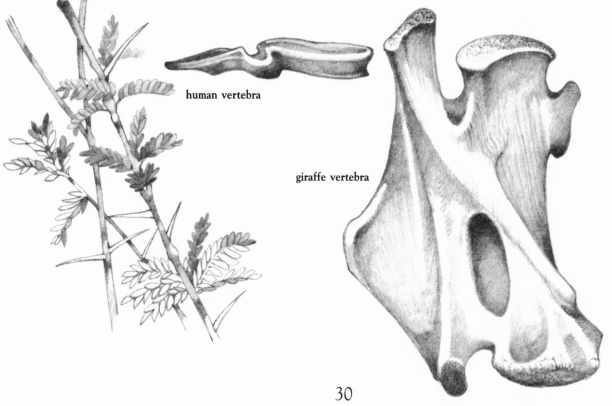

human vertebra

giraffe vertebra

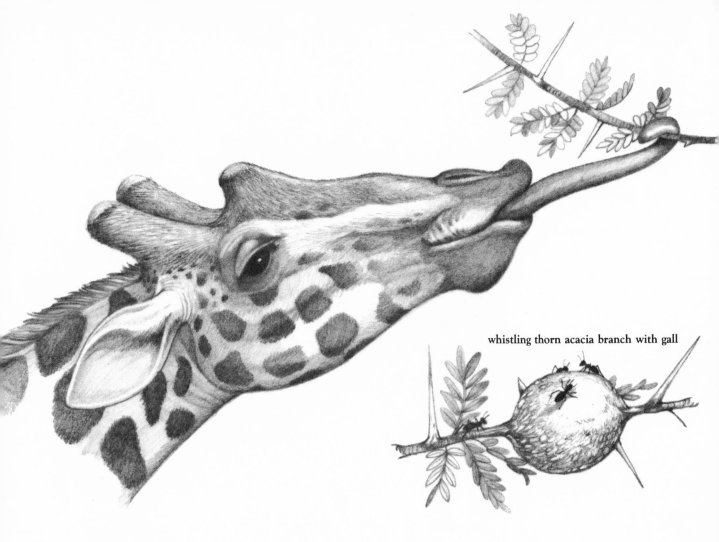

whistling thorn acacia branch with gall

Acacia leaves are 74 percent water, and when giraffes are grazing on them, they can go a long time without drinking. Since giraffes don't sweat or pant to cool off, they don't require a lot of water. They control their body temperature through their very thick skin and the size and shape of their bodies. Although their temperature may rise two or three degrees on hot days, they cool off quickly when the temperature drops after sunset. Their long, thin legs and neck surfaces release heat rapidly.

If water is plentiful, giraffes usually drink at least once every three days. In three days they can travel a long way to find it, if necessary. When water is scarce, they rely on morning dew and the moisture content of their food. This ability allows them to browse in semiarid regions far from water, where most other animals cannot.

Giraffes are reluctant to visit waterholes, and they drink only when they are absolutely sure no danger is lurking nearby. One giraffe rarely goes to a waterhole alone. It joins several others. They may spend an hour or more carefully inspecting the surroundings before moving on to the waterhole. While one drinks, the others line up, patiently waiting their turn. A giraffe can drink up to ten gallons of water. It drinks for a few seconds, straightens up, then drinks again five or six times before getting its fill. At least one giraffe keeps watch at all times. Wildebeests and gazelles form another line and join the giraffes at the waterhole, knowing it is safe for them to drink while the keen-sighted animals are there to serve as lookouts.

When drinking or licking salt, a giraffe is very awkward. Though its neck is long enough to reach the top of a tree, it is too short to reach the ground. To drink, a giraffe must either bend its forelegs, spiderlike, or spread them apart by a series of jerks. Either position is very dangerous because the giraffe is helpless if attacked by a predator. It can rise very suddenly if necessary, however, by snapping its head back and at the same time straightening its forelegs and pulling them together.

A giraffe's stomach is divided into four compartments like that of a cow. Water passes directly into the second stomach. Food goes into the first stomach, which is a sort of storage tank. Giraffes eat a lot, very fast, without taking time to chew it. Twigs, leaves, thorns, pods, and fruit are all briefly mixed together with saliva and swallowed whole. In the first stomach (the rumen) the food is mixed with gastric juices and partly fermented. Then, during the heat of the day while the animal rests, the food is formed into round, fist-sized lumps or cuds, which are brought back up into the mouth to be thoroughly chewed. This ruminating takes a lot of time. The giraffe chews each cud for about a minute, rotating its jaws to grind the cud between the ridged, washboard-like molars at the back of its mouth. Then it swallows the ground-up cud and immediately brings up another.

The chewed cud goes into the large third stomach. There the first stages of digestion take place, and water is absorbed before the food passes into the fourth stomach, where it is completely digested.

During the day adults usually stand close together while resting and ruminating. At night they may rest lying down, but only if they feel that it is completely safe. A herd never lies down all at the same time. At least one giraffe is always on guard. To lie down, giraffes fold their forelegs and tuck their hind legs under their bodies. Their necks remain upright most of the time. Lying flat gives giraffes indigestion, because, as in all ruminants, the force of gravity is needed to move food from one stomach to another in the digestive process. Giraffes may doze with their eyes alternately open and closed, but they remain alert. Their ears are constantly moving, listening for danger. They sleep deeply only four or five minutes at a time and only for a total of half an hour a day. When sleeping soundly, a giraffe lays its neck along its back with its head on its flank or rests it in the crotch of a tree.

For a giraffe, getting back up from a lying position is very difficult. It uses its neck as a counterbalance, throwing the neck back to lift itself into a kneeling position on its forelegs. Then, swinging the neck slightly backward and vigorously forward, it raises its rear quarters over its hind feet. Finally the neck is drawn well back again, removing the weight from the forelegs so the giraffe can straighten them and stand upright. Not only does this take considerable effort, but it also takes a good while to accomplish. The only time a giraffe is more vulnerable to attack by predators is right after birth.

reticulated giraffe mother and newborn calf

5
The Birth of a Giraffe

To have her baby, a mother giraffe chooses a spot that is free of underbrush and tall grass in which a predator might hide. She carefully looks around and turns her ears in every direction. When convinced that no lions, leopards, or hyenas are lurking about, she spreads her legs and bends her knees to lessen the baby's fall. The five-foot drop stuns the new baby giraffe, but it revives quickly as its mother licks it dry, removing the odors that might attract predators. She gently nudges it with her soft nose until it skillfully scrambles onto its wobbly legs. Although the newborn is only a few minutes old, it knows how to accomplish this difficult task.

Most giraffe cows prefer to give birth alone, but some choose to do so in the middle of the herd, where there is better protection. Birth is the most dangerous time in a giraffe's life. Predators kill more than half of the babies in the first few minutes after their birth. Those born during the heat of the day while predators sleep are safest.

A healthy calf stands within ten minutes after its birth and is usually nursing within an hour. Four teats are located on the mother's underside just in front of her hind legs. To nurse, the baby must spread its legs far apart, lower its long neck, and turn its head almost upside down. It nurses gustily with loud smacking noises. The rich, sweet milk makes the baby strong. When the mother thinks it has had enough, she simply walks away, leaving it to follow her.

A newborn is six and a half feet tall and weighs 120 to 150 pounds. Its neck is much shorter than its mother's— only one-sixth as long as the baby's total height, while its mother's neck is one-third of her height. Its hoofs are soft but harden quickly. Its horns, which are small cartilage bumps with long tassels of black hair, lie flat because they are not fastened to the skull at birth. However, the horns are standing erect within a week.

The baby's hair is soft and woolly, its dark mane thick and bristly. Its spots are paler than they will be when it is grown, but its spot pattern is permanent. Each giraffe has a unique neck pattern that distinguishes it from all others, a pattern as distinctive as fingerprints for a human. Scientists use these patterns to identify individual giraffes, and giraffes may also use them to identify one another.

A baby giraffe is vulnerable to attack while the mother feeds. Although it can run and jump within ten hours, it cannot run fast enough to outrun a predator. So the giraffe cow hides her calf in tall grass or a nearby thicket while she browses or drinks. As long as the baby lies still with its head on its rump, it is reasonably safe. It is camouflaged by its dark spots and creamy background.

The mother returns often to let her baby nurse during the first week after birth. After that she returns only three or four times a day. When the cow reappears, the calf remains still until she carefully inspects the area for signs

Masai giraffe mother and nursing calf

of danger. When convinced all is safe, she nudges the calf and licks its neck; only then does it nurse.

The baby remains hidden for a month. The mother may browse several miles away, but the calf waits patiently for her return, moving very little. It grows quickly and gains strength. As soon as it can outrun a lion and is bigger than a cheetah, it is relatively safe from predators. Although a cheetah can outrun a grown giraffe, it seldom attacks animals bigger than itself.

A mother giraffe is affectionate and protective toward her baby, touching, rubbing, licking, and sniffing it. Normally gentle, she can be quite vicious in defending her young. She delivers savage downward chops with her forefeet and crushing blows with her hind feet that can kill a lion. When frightened, the baby hides under its mother's belly.

When a calf is a month old, the mother and calf join four or five other cows with calves. Each morning the cows take their calves to a special nursery area, usually a clearing on a knoll. They eat together for a while; then one by one the cows leave. The calves lie down or nibble acacia bushes very near the place where they were left. If frightened, they may run off together but always circle back to the nursery area when the danger passes. Sometimes one mother remains with the calves to "baby-sit" them. Scientists are not certain how giraffes determine which cow will be the sitter, but it appears that the mothers may take turns. Occasionally the calves seem to be tended by an "auntie," a female too old to bear young of her own.

Although the mothers may browse fifteen miles away, each returns several times a day to nurse her young. After nursing, the mothers leave again but return at dusk to protect the calves during the night. The calves stay in these nursery groups until they are a year old.

Two-month-old calves rest no more than five hours a day. They play tag and follow the leader, games that teach them necessary living skills. They frisk, buck, gallop, and jump. When they get tired, they flop to the ground for a few minutes, then are up again exploring their world. Like all baby animals, they are extremely curious and venturesome. Mother giraffes are constantly alert for danger. When concerned for their young's safety, they call them back with a soft whistling sound.

Calves start browsing when they are two weeks old and are nibbling whistling thorn within a month. They begin chewing cuds when they are four months old. Once they

have started eating acacia leaves, calves need little milk. They continue to nurse, however, until they are at least a year old because they can't drink water. Their necks are too short to reach it, even if they knew how to bend their knees or splay their legs apart. Calves have to learn how to do this tricky maneuver. Sometimes they get into ridiculous and complicated positions attempting it. Fortunately they get all the moisture they need from milk and plants until their necks grow long enough and they have mastered this procedure.

Calves grow rapidly during their first year. They may gain an inch or more a day the first week and four feet the first year. Four-month-olds can take care of themselves. By the time they are a year old, they are ten- to twelve-foot teenagers. They reach maturity at four years but continue to grow until they are seven or eight years old. Females will be fourteen to sixteen feet tall (tall enough to look into a second-story window) and weigh from eighteen hundred to two thousand pounds. Males grow to be sixteen to eighteen feet tall and weigh up to three thousand pounds. The tallest giraffe on record was nineteen feet tall.

Giraffes usually have one calf every two years. Normally a female has her first calf when she is five years old and can reproduce until she is twenty. Mother giraffes nuzzle their two-year-old calves but no longer take care of them. Males seldom run with cows and calves except at mating time.

Courtship is usually brief, without much display. The male follows the female around for a day or so and courts her by entwining and rubbing his neck against hers. Babies arrive fifteen months after their parents mated and may be born any time of the year.

Masai giraffe herd, running

6
Fight or Flee

Strutting up to the leader of the herd, a young bull curves his neck and dips his head in an invitation to duel. Accepting the challenge, the old bull returns the bow. The challenger then swings back his head and slams his horns into the other's belly. Thus begins a fifteen-minute bout in which the two bulls pound each other with their massive heads. Finally the young male has had enough and gallops off into the bush.

Such encounters occur daily in giraffe country. Although the blows may land anywhere on the body, these bouts are called "neck-knocking" because the giraffes use their necks as well as their heads as weapons. The males aren't defending territories or fighting for mates. Their sparring matches are used to determine rank in the herd. The dominant male is the strongest and usually the largest. He gets first choice of females and food.

An old male's head makes a formidable weapon. It may weigh more than twenty-five pounds. The skull bones are thickened from constant battering. A bull's head is often four or five times heavier than a female's.

Bulls never bite or kick during neck-knocking bouts. Though the sledgehammer blows must hurt, injuries are rare. Giraffe horns are blunt, and an old male's skin is tough—tougher than any other animal's—and may be up to an inch thick. Once they have determined who is strongest, males live together peacefully, rubbing necks and grazing side by side.

45

GEORGE ROGERS CLARK
LIBRARY MEDIA CENTER

reticulated male

Giraffe horns, which are properly called ossicones (OS-see-kones), are not true horns like those of cattle or antelopes. They are covered with skin and hair. The cartilage present at birth is gradually replaced by bone, and the horns grow in size, eventually fusing to the skull at the age of four to four and a half years in males and a little over seven years in females. The horns of bull giraffes are nine inches long and are thick and cylindrical. They continue to grow bigger around as long as the giraffe lives. The knobbed ends are usually bare because sparring wears the hair off. The horns of females are only half as long as the males'. They are tapered and tipped with tufts of black hair.

All giraffes have at least two horns. Reticulated and Masai males have a third bumplike horn between their eyes. In females this horn is very small or missing. These center horns fuse even later than the main horns. Rothschild's giraffes have two additional horns.

female

male, fully developed

The horns are never used in defense. Giraffes prefer walking away from trouble to fighting. If cornered, however, they fight with their hoofs. Their strong legs and huge feet can be deadly weapons when needed.

Adult giraffes are relatively safe when standing; their bodies are well above a predator's reach. A leopard may occasionally drop out of a tree onto a giraffe, and sometimes a lion leaps onto a giraffe's back, but this action is rare. Whenever it does happen, the giraffe brushes the animal off by galloping through the tallest bush it can find. The cat's claws may leave long scars on the giraffe's rump, but the giraffe survives.

A giraffe's feet and legs are even better suited for running than for fighting, and for a giraffe, speed is the most effective defense. Giraffes seldom need to run far because lions don't depend upon speed to catch prey. They usually hunt in groups and wait in ambush.

fetlock ▶

viewed from below

giraffe forefoot

Giraffes' wedge-shaped hoofs are designed for carrying great weight and are different from those of any other ungulate. The hoofs are four to six inches high in front and so low at the back that the fetlocks nearly touch the ground. The forefeet are slightly larger than the hind feet because they support most of the weight of the neck and head.

The six-foot-long forelegs appear to be much longer than the hind legs, but they are actually only slightly longer. They look longer because the giraffe's back slopes from twelve feet at the withers (top of the shoulders) to eight feet at the rump in males, and from eight to six and a half feet in females. Much of the slope is due to the very long spines on the vertebrae at the base of the neck, which anchor the heavy muscles supporting the neck and head. The giraffe's shoulder blades—the longest and narrowest found in any living mammal—also contribute to the slope. The sloping back allows the hind legs to support part of the weight of the neck and head.

Giraffes walk differently from most animals because their legs are nearly twice as long as their bodies. To keep from stepping on its forefeet with its hind feet, a giraffe moves the two legs on its right side forward as a pair, then brings forward the two legs on its left side. The neck and head move back and forth twice during each stride. The neck movement propels the giraffe forward and helps it keep its balance.

When walking away from trouble, giraffes appear to be moving very slowly because they take only one stride every two seconds. Actually they are moving quite rapidly—about ten miles per hour—because they cover fifteen feet with each step. They can be out of danger within seconds.

When alarmed, a giraffe curls its tail over its back, pushes off with its front legs, and gallops away. All four legs bunch together underneath the animal, then spread. Head and neck pump back and forth, shifting the weight alternately from front to back. A giraffe can plunge into a gallop instantly, even from a resting position. It is able to gallop thirty-five miles per hour for short distances and maintain up to thirty-two miles per hour for great distances over any kind of country.

A healthy giraffe can outrun a horse but gets winded more quickly and takes longer to recover. Although a giraffe's lungs are powerful and about eight times larger than

a human's lungs, they must work harder to pull air down the long windpipe. A giraffe breathes only eight to ten times a minute, which helps to lessen the load on the lungs. Giraffe blood is not much different from human blood, except that it has more oxygen-carrying red corpuscles and takes up oxygen more rapidly.

Giraffes are easily panicked, and an animal that runs too far may die of a heart attack. A giraffe's heart is two feet long and weighs twenty-four pounds, which is .8 percent of its total body weight—about the same as a cow's heart. A giraffe's heart is more powerful than a cow's because it must work harder. A cow's brain is only a foot above its heart. A bull giraffe's heart must pump blood up ten feet to its brain. It pumps twenty gallons of blood per minute and beats 150 times. A giraffe's blood pressure at heart level is higher than that of any other animal—more than twice as high as a human's blood pressure. At brain level, however, the pressure is the same as a human's. The arteries have thick walls to withstand such pressure, and thick, tight skin on the giraffe's slender legs helps to maintain it. Special control valves in the arteries of the neck and a network of blood vessels in the head prevent the blood from rushing to the brain when the giraffe lowers its head to drink or feed from ground level.

Valves in blood vessels in the neck control blood pressure when the giraffe lowers or raises its head.

As soon as they are old enough to outrun predators, most giraffes don't try to conceal themselves, even though their coloring camouflages them very effectively when they stand among yellow-barked acacia trees. When they sense danger, they prefer to peer above a bush or around a tree and get a better view. If they tried to hide, their rapidly swishing tails would probably give them away.

Scientists think giraffes whisk their tails to alert others to danger. Giraffes also use a variety of sounds to communicate. They snort, grunt, moo, and whistle. Scientists aren't sure what all these sounds mean.

Color and color patterns distinguish one giraffe from another and vary a great deal from subspecies to subspecies and from individual to individual. Although rare, all white, all black, and all light brown giraffes have been seen. Most giraffes have a light background with dark spots. The background color varies from creamy white to almost yellow. The spots range from light chestnut to liver-colored to almost black, getting darker as the animal ages.

The shape and size of a giraffe's spots are used to determine its subspecies. Giraffes may be reticulated or blotched. Reticulated giraffes have large straight-edged spots that are placed close together with only a narrow network of ground color between. *Reticulated* means "marked like network," and reticulated giraffes look as if they are covered with a cream-colored net. The width of the network varies from one subspecies to another.

Blotched giraffes are covered with irregularly shaped spots separated by broad bands of lighter background color. The spots may be leaf-shaped, jagged, or smooth-edged. Hybrids resulting from interbreeding of subspecies have an even greater variety of color and spots.

Giraffe hair is short and smooth, like that of a horse. In spite of the thick red dust that settles on everything on the

reticulated (reticulated) ▶

Nubian (reticulated) ▶

southern (blotched) ▶

Masai (blotched) ▶

hot, dry savannas, giraffes look very clean even though they never go into the water to bathe. They clean themselves and one another by scratching and licking. They rub their necks and heads on their rumps or on tree trunks and branches to remove caked dirt and ticks. They straddle bushes or termite hills and rock back and forth to clean their bellies. They clean their nostrils and ears with their tongues and comb out the long hairs of their tails with their teeth.

Birds called oxpeckers often run up and down giraffes' necks and backs, eating ticks and other insects that pester giraffes and clearing their hides of dirt, bits of dry skin, and loose hair.

Good grooming keeps giraffes healthy and helps them live long lives. Scientists estimate the age of giraffes up to six years old by their tooth eruption pattern. Six-and-a-half-year-olds have all of their teeth. Scientists use photographs to help them keep track of the age of giraffes that are older than six and a half. If a scientist knows when the picture was made, and the approximate age of the giraffe at that time, he can figure out how long the animal has lived. In captivity at least one giraffe lived to be thirty years of age. The oldest known wild giraffe was a twenty-eight-year-old male. It is rare for a wild giraffe to die of old age. When giraffes become old and weak, they usually are taken by predators.

7

The Future for Giraffes

Although giraffes once roamed all of Africa, there are fewer than one hundred thousand surviving on only 10 percent of the continent today. There probably never were huge numbers at any one time, because the ecology of the region could not support large herds and giraffes rarely overpopulate an area, but there have been many more than there are now. Giraffes have been declining in numbers for at least six thousand years, but the process has increased drastically in the last two hundred years.

Disease and climatic changes contributed to the decline, but human greed is responsible for much of the recent acceleration. Many giraffes were shot, some because they tore down telegraph lines, some because they trampled crops, others for food or for their tails, but most were shot for sport. By 1900 giraffes were almost extinct.

When it became obvious that the giraffe population was in serious danger, people throughout the world united to help save the giraffes. Much has been accomplished. African governments began to recognize giraffes as valuable natural resources and passed laws making it illegal to kill them. Hunting for sport was stopped, railroad companies began using taller poles to lift telegraph wires out of the giraffes' reach, and farmers electrified their fences to prevent giraffes from jumping them.

These measures haven't completely stopped the killing, however, and they haven't solved all of the giraffes' problems. The biggest difficulty facing them today is lack of space. Giraffes require large browsing ranges, and these are becoming hard to find. The number of people in Africa is growing very rapidly; in some countries it is doubling every year. These people need more and more room. They clear trees from the land to grow food or to build factories, leaving less space for giraffes and other wild animals.

Africans are fond of giraffes and are working hard to coexist with them. Many nations have set aside large areas as national parks and game preserves, where animals are protected and can live without danger. Others have moved giraffe herds from highly populated areas to regions suitable for giraffes, but not for farming. In addition, many farmers are allowing giraffes to run on their cattle ranches because they keep the acacia trees pruned back, allowing more grass to grow; because they don't interfere with livestock; and because they seldom eat crops.

These measures have greatly benefited the giraffes. They are not in danger of extinction at present. Their numbers have stabilized; about as many are born each year as die. However, another problem brought about by increasing human populations could again threaten their existence. There is a great deal of meat on a giraffe, and there are a large number of poor and hungry people in Africa. Even though it is against the law to kill a giraffe in most African countries, hungry people kill them anyway. Game rangers patrol the national parks to prevent poaching (illegal killing), but there are too few rangers to stop it entirely.

To solve the problem of feeding the hungry, government officials are looking into the possibility of raising giraffes for meat. Although the meat is tough, many Africans consider it delicious. Giraffes are more efficient than cattle. They eat vegetation no other animals do; they require less water and can live in drier climates; and they produce much more meat. Free-roaming herds would require no care except culling once a year. Therefore giraffes would be a cheap source of protein.

Very little of the giraffe would be wasted. The skin makes excellent shoes, harnesses, whips, and shields. Tails are highly prized as flyswatters, and the long hairs are made into good-luck bracelets that are worn by the African people or sold to tourists.

Tourism is one of the most important industries in many African countries. Every year thousands of people from around the world go there to shoot the animals with cameras instead of guns. Tourists are especially partial to the beautiful giraffes. Tourism may be an important factor in the survival of these magnificent animals because it prompts governments to work harder to find ways to save them.

Scientists are trying to learn what giraffes need to survive, but these animals are not easy to study. It is very difficult to follow a single giraffe for several days. It can go through areas a jeep can't and is able to travel much faster than a human on foot. It may cover as much as twenty-five miles in a single day and quickly become lost to sight in the brush. The only way to learn where a giraffe goes is to outfit it with a radio transmitter, but a giraffe won't allow humans to get close enough to attach one. Scientists have tried shooting an animal with tranquilizing bullets, then fastening the collar around its neck, but this is a risky business because giraffes have delicate nervous systems. Other scientists are trying to determine the population densities by counting the number of giraffes in each area. A tally is made both from the air and by land. Many people are photographing individuals so that they can identify them and learn where they go and which other giraffes they associate with. Although much has been learned, a great deal more has yet to be discovered if these gentle giants are to be saved.

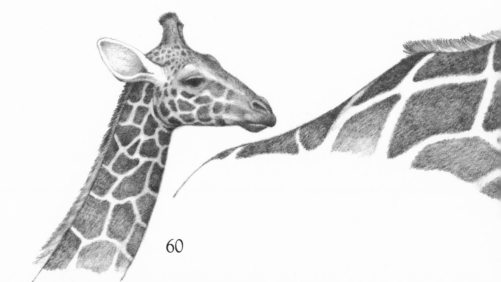

We have much to learn from giraffes. These unique creatures are the result of millions of years of evolution. If we follow their example by learning to adapt to our environment without destroying it, by managing our population growth so that we do not overpopulate the earth, and by coexisting peacefully with every species (including our own), then our kind too might expect to exist for millions of years.

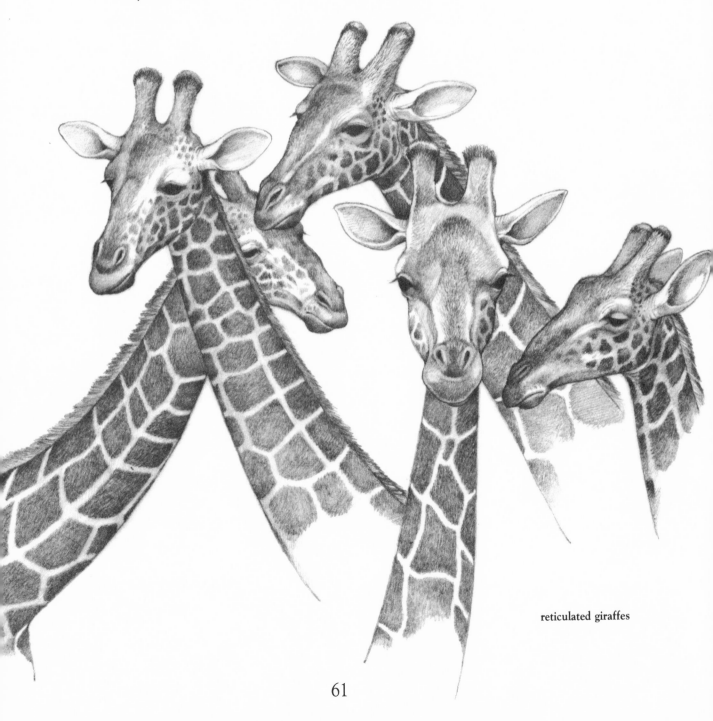

reticulated giraffes

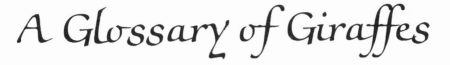

A Glossary of Giraffes

Angolan giraffe

ANGOLAN GIRAFFE (*Giraffa camelopardalis angolensis*)—A giraffe race or subspecies found only in Angola, northern Namibia, and Zambia. Its small, smooth-edged, slightly notched spots are spaced far apart and extend to the hoofs.

BARINGO GIRAFFE—*See* ROTHSCHILD'S GIRAFFE.

BIRGERBOHLINIA ("Birger Bohlin's giraffid")—An extinct genus of the Sivatheriinae family that lived in southern Europe during the Pleistocene epoch. This animal had a short neck and two large ossicones similar to those of a giraffe.

BRAMATHERIUM ("Brama beast")—A genus of gigantic, short-necked, late Pliocene sivatheres that lived in Asia. It had a short face, heavy neck muscles, short legs, and four large, conical ossicones, two pointing upward and two projecting toward the sides.

CAPE GIRAFFE—*See* SOUTHERN GIRAFFE.

CHAD GIRAFFE—*See* NIGERIAN GIRAFFE.

Bramatherium

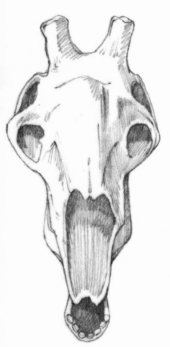

GIRAFFA ("Giraffe")—A genus of long-necked, long-legged Giraffinae that has existed in Africa and Europe from the late Miocene to the present. It first appeared in Africa and spread to Eurasia during the Pliocene, where it persisted until the early Pleistocene. The only living species is *G. camelopardalis*. Extinct species include *G. attica*, *G. jumae*, *G. priscilla*, *G. punjabiensis*, *G. sivalensis*, and *G. stillei*.

G. attica skull

GIRAFFA ATTICA ("Giraffe from Attica")— An early Pliocene species of *Giraffa* that lived in Greece and Turkey. It somewhat resembled the modern giraffe but was much smaller. It was probably closely related to *G. sivalensis* and *G. stillei*.

GIRAFFA CAMELOPARDALIS (Modern giraffe)—This is the scientific name of the modern giraffe, the only living species of Giraffinae. There is some disagreement among authorities as to the number of subspecies of *G. camelopardalis*, but these nine are the most widely accepted: Angolan, Kordofan, Masai, Nigerian, Nubian, reticulated, Rothschild's, southern, and Thornicroft's. Some would add Congoenesis, but others believe this is the same as the Nubian.

GIRAFFA JUMAE ("Juma's giraffe")—The oldest known species of *Giraffa*. It lived in east Africa from the late Miocene to the mid-Pleistocene. This two-horned giraffid was probably closely related to the modern giraffe, which it resembled. It was about the same size, but its ossicones sloped more steeply backward.

G. jumae

GIRAFFA PRISCILLA ("Priscilla's giraffe")—
This species is thought by some to be the earliest Asiatic *Giraffa*, but its status is not certain because its canine teeth have not been found. It was smaller than other *Giraffa* species. It lived in India during the early Pliocene.

GIRAFFA PUNJABIENSIS ("Giraffe from Punjab")—A *Giraffa* species that lived in India during the middle Pliocene. It was smaller than G. *camelopardalis* and possibly smaller than G. *stillei*.

GIRAFFA SIVALENSIS ("Giraffe from Siva-lik")—An early Pleistocene *Giraffa* that lived in India. It was larger than G. *punjabiensis* but slightly smaller than G. *camelopardalis*.

GIRAFFA STILLEI ("Stille's giraffe")—A small species of *Giraffa* that lived in east Africa from the early Pliocene to the middle Pleistocene. It had slender ossicones.

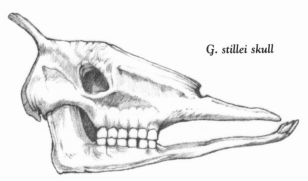

G. stillei skull

GIRAFFIDAE—A family of even-toed, cud-chewing hoofed animals with two-bladed canine teeth and ridged molars. Some had ossicones, some did not. They are commonly called giraffids.

GIRAFFINAE—A subfamily of medium- to large-sized, long-necked, long-legged giraffids. Their forelegs are longer than the hind, and their conical horns (properly called ossicones) are bony extensions of the skull covered with skin and hair. *Giraffa* and *Honanotherium* are genera of Giraffinae.

GIRAFFINE—*See* GIRAFFINAE.

GIRAFFOKERYX ("Giraffe forerunner")—A medium-sized sivathere with four large ossicones—one pair above the eyes and one pair at the back of the skull. It was common in Asia during the Miocene and lived in east Africa from the mid-Miocene to the mid-Pliocene. It was about the size of an okapi.

Giraffokeryx

HELLADOTHERIUM ("Beast from Greece")—

A hornless, short-necked, moose-sized sivathere that lived in Europe and Asia during the late Miocene and early Pliocene. It had a rump like an ox's, short, sturdy legs, a huge, twenty-seven-inch head, and either very small ossicones or none at all.

Helladotherium

HONANOTHERIUM ("Beast from Honan Province")—

A genus of Giraffinae that lived in China during the middle Pliocene. It is known from several teeth that are larger than those of the modern giraffe.

KORDOFAN GIRAFFE (*Giraffa camelopardalis antiquorum*)—

A reticulated giraffe subspecies with small, smooth-edged, somewhat irregularly shaped spots separated by wide webbing. The legs are spotted on the inner sides to the hocks. Most of the few surviving members of this three-horned race live in the Garamba National Park in Zaire.

Kordofan giraffe

67

MASAI GIRAFFE (*Giraffa camelopardalis tippels-kirchi*)—A giraffe subspecies that has large, leafy spots extending down to the hoofs. The spots vary in shape and color within a herd. This giraffe is not endangered at this time. Large numbers live in Tanzania and Kenya.

Nigerian giraffe

Masai giraffe

NIGERIAN GIRAFFE (*Giraffa camelopardalis peralta*)—Also called the Chad giraffe or the West African giraffe. This reticulated subspecies of giraffes has relatively pale, more or less smooth-edged but irregularly shaped spots divided by broad webbing and extending below the hocks. These large giraffes once ranged over wide areas of western Africa but are now nearly extinct because of climatic changes and geographic barriers that prevent them from migrating. A few live in Yakari Game Range in Nigeria.

NUBIAN GIRAFFE (*Giraffa camelopardalis camelopardalis*)

—This subspecies was the first giraffe scientifically described. It is similar to the reticulated giraffe, but its smooth-edged, irregularly shaped spots have fuzzier edges and are separated by wider buffy white webbings. The inner sides of the legs are unspotted and are pure white below the hocks. This race is fairly common in eastern Sudan bordering Ethiopia.

Nubian spot pattern

okapi

OKAPI (*Okapia johnstoni*)

—This giraffid, whose name comes from African words meaning "forest giraffe," is the only living relative of the giraffe. It is generally considered to be a paleotragine, but recent studies suggest it may be a giraffine. Instead of spots, it has a dark coat with white stripes like those of a zebra on the rump and legs. The females are larger than the males and hornless. The spike-like ossicones of the males are covered with hair except for the pointed tips. Okapi feed alone at night. They live only in the rain forests of Zaire and are an endangered species.

PALEOMERYCIDAE—A family of small, even-toed, deerlike ruminants, some of which had branching ossicones. The ancestors of giraffids, as well as those of deer and antelope, may have come from this group.

PALEOTRAGINAE—A subfamily of primitive giraffids. Except for the okapi, all known species lived during the Miocene. These were the smallest giraffids. They had two ossicones, well developed in males and small or absent in females. Their necks and legs were elongated but not so much as those of modern giraffes. They lived in Africa and Eurasia. Genera include *Okapia*, *Paleotragus*, *Samotherium*, and *Zarafa*.

PALEOTRAGINE—*See* PALEOTRAGINAE.

PALEOTRAGUS ("Ancient goat")—A genus of small to large Paleotraginae that lived in Europe, Asia, and Africa during the Miocene epoch. These giraffids were built much like an okapi and may have been direct ancestors of that animal. They were six to thirteen feet tall. Males had a single pair of simple spikelike ossicones.

RETICULATED GIRAFFE (*Giraffa camelopardalis reticulata*)—A giraffe subspecies with large, smooth-edged, closely spaced spots separated by only a fine network of light color. The spots extend below the hocks. About four hundred reticulated giraffes exist in the Samburu Game Reserve in Kenya.

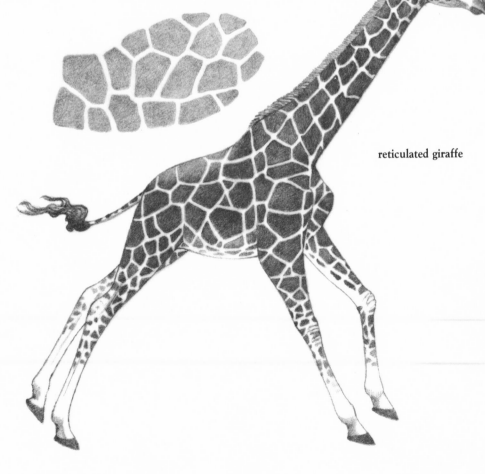

reticulated giraffe

ROTHSCHILD'S GIRAFFE (*Giraffa camelopardalis rothschildi*)—Also called Baringo giraffe and Uganda giraffe. A reticulated subspecies with smooth-edged, fanlike spots separated by wider white lines than those of the reticulated giraffe and extending well below the hocks. Old males have five horns—two small extra horns behind the two main ossicones. Fewer than two hundred live in Kenya, and fewer than nine hundred in Kidepo Valley National Park in Uganda.

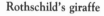

Rothschild's giraffe

SAMOTHERIUM ("Beast from the Isle of Samos")—A genus of Paleotraginae that lived in Greece, India, and Africa from fifteen to five million years ago. This medium-sized, large-bodied giraffid had elongated neck and legs and two simple pointed ossicones.

SIVATHERES—*See* SIVATHERIINAE.

African *Sivatherium*

SIVATHERIINAE—A subfamily of heavy giraffids, commonly called sivatheres. They lived in Europe, Asia, and Africa from fifteen million to five thousand years ago. They were gigantic, short-necked giraffids with rumps like those of oxen and sturdy legs like those of cattle. Some lacked ossicones, but most had two pairs that were usually larger than those of the giraffines. Some of the ossicones were huge and oddly shaped. *Birgerbohlinia*, *Bramatherium*, *Giraffokeryx*, *Helladotherium*, and *Sivatherium* are genera of Sivatheriinae.

European *Sivatherium*

SIVATHERIUM ("Siva's beast")—This giraffid was the largest of the sivatheres. Its fossils have been found in India and Africa. The African species (*S. maurusium*) was ten feet tall. Its body was as big as that of a modern giraffe, but its neck and legs were shorter. It was slightly smaller than the Asian species (*S. giganteum*). Both species had thick, sturdy legs like those of cattle and a short, massive neck to support the weight of four ossicones—two similar to those of the modern giraffe and two heavy, ornate weapons that resembled those of a moose. Species of *Sivatherium* lived from the middle Pliocene to about five thousand years ago.

SOUTH AFRICAN GIRAFFE—*See* SOUTHERN GIRAFFE.

SOUTHERN GIRAFFE (*Giraffa camelopardalis giraffa*)—Also called Cape giraffe or South African giraffe. This giraffe subspecies has large, widely separated, roughly rounded splotches that sometimes have delicate needlelike extensions. It lives in a colder climate than the other giraffes and has longer hair. It rarely has more than two horns. Females have only two teats. This race lives in dry, uncultivated areas of Namibia, Botswana, eastern South Africa, southwest Mozambique, and the western part of Zimbabwe.

THORNICROFT'S GIRAFFE *(Giraffa camelopardalis thornicrofti)*—A giraffe subspecies with spots almost starlike in shape that become oblong and lighter in color on the neck. The legs are spotted to the hoofs. The few hundred surviving Thornicroft's giraffes live in northern Zimbabwe.

Thornicroft's giraffe

UGANDA GIRAFFE—*See* ROTHSCHILD'S GIRAFFE.

WEST AFRICAN GIRAFFE—*See* NIGERIAN GIRAFFE.

ZARAFA ("Tallest animal")—This six-foot giraffid was the earliest known paleotragine. It lived in northern Africa during the early Miocene. It had a flat forehead and spikelike ossicones projecting straight out on each side.

Zarafa

A Geological Timetable
for Giraffes

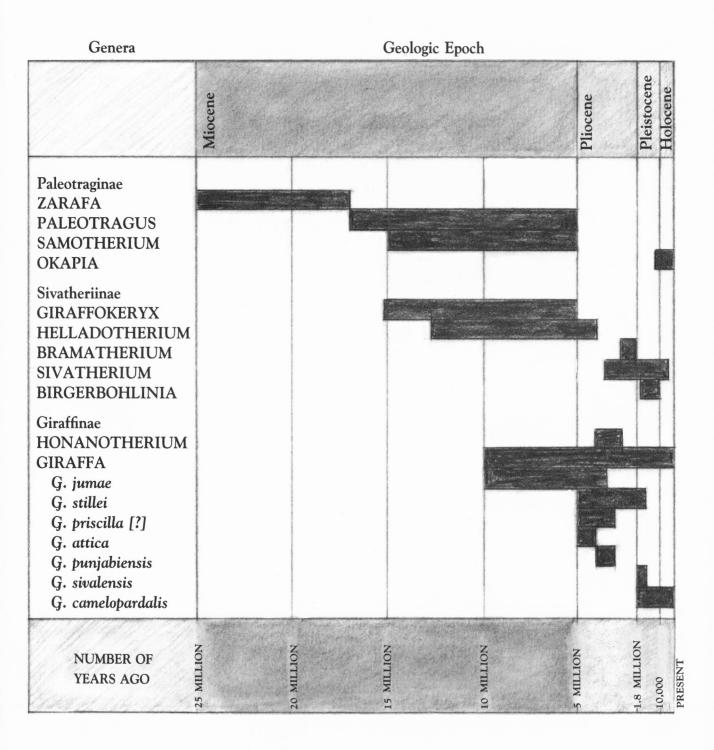

Classification of Giraffids

Scientists classify all living things by grouping those closely related into families and then dividing families into genera and species. Many species of giraffids are known from very fragmentary material, and the relationships among them are not clear. The genera in this chart are listed in the order of their appearance in the fossil record. In the Glossary they are listed alphabetically. Species are listed only for living genera.

Family—Giraffidae (jye-RAF-ih-dee)

Subfamily—Paleotraginae (PAY-lee-o-TRAG-ih-nee)

Genera

Zarafa (zah-RAHF-ah)

Paleotragus (PAY-lee-o-TRAG-us)

Samotherium (sam-o-THEE-rih-um)

Okapia (o-KAH-pee-ah)

Subfamily—Sivatheriinae (siv-ah-THEE-ree-ih-nee)

Genera

Giraffokeryx (jye-raf-foh-KER-iks)

Helladotherium (HEL-lah-doh-THEE-rih-um)

Sivatherium (siv-ah-THEE-rih-um)

Bramatherium (brah-mah-THEE-rih-um)

Birgerbohlinia (BIR-jer-bow-LIH-nee-ah)

Subfamily—Giraffinae (jye-RAF-fih-nee)

Genera

Honanotherium (HOE-nan-o-THEE-rih-um)

Giraffa (jye-RAHF-fa)

Species

G. *jumae* (JEW-me)

G. *stillei* (STIL-eye)

G. *priscilla* (prih-SIL-ah)

G. *attica* (AT-tih-ka)

G. *punjabiensis* (pun-jab-EN-sis)

G. *sivalensis* (siv-ah-LEN-sis)

G. *camelopardalis* (KAM-el-o-par-DAL-is)

Subspecies

Angolan (G. *c. angolensis*)

Kordofan (G. *c. antiquorum*)

Masai (G. *c. tippelskirchi*)

Nigerian (G. *c. peralta*)

Nubian (G. *c. camelopardalis*)

reticulated (G. *c. reticulata*)

Rothschild's (G. *c. rothschildi*)

For Further Reading

Arnold, Caroline. *Giraffe*. New York: William Morrow & Company, 1987.

Dagg, Anne Innis. "Giraffe Movement and the Neck." *Natural History*, August/September 1962, 45–50.

———, and J. Bristol Foster. *The Giraffe: Its Biology, Behavior and Ecology*. Malabar, Florida: Robert E. Krieger Publishing Company, 1982.

Foster, Bristol. "Africa's Gentle Giants." *National Geographic*, September 1977, 402–17.

Frame, George W. "Giraffes—Neck-knockers of Africa." *Science Digest*, August 1973, 64–68.

Langman, Vaughan A. "Giraffe Youngsters Need a Little Bit of Maternal Love." *Smithsonian*, January 1982, 95–139.

MacClintock, Dorcas. *A Natural History of Giraffes*. New York: Charles Scribner's Sons, 1973.

Moss, Cynthia. *Portraits of the Wild*. Boston: Houghton Mifflin Company, 1975.

Patterson, Carolyn Bennett. "Rescuing the Rothschild." *National Geographic*, September 1977, 419–21.

Spinage, C. A. *The Book of the Giraffe*. Boston: Houghton Mifflin Company, 1968.

Warren, James V. "The Physiology of the Giraffe." *Scientific American*, November 1974, 96–105.

Wexo, John Bennett. *Giraffes*. San Diego, California: Wildlife Education, Ltd., 1982.